D0912975

CHILDREN 636.72 LANDAU 2011
Landau, Elaine
Boston terriers are the
  best!

Central   08/08/2011

CENTRAL LIBRARY

THE BEST
DOGS
EVER

BOSTON TERRIERS ARE THE BEST!

Elaine Landau

LERNER PUBLICATIONS COMPANY · MINNEAPOLIS

FORT WORTH LIBRARY

For Barbara Genco

Copyright © 2011 by Lerner Publishing Group, Inc.

All rights reserved. International copyright secured. No part of this book
may be reproduced, stored in a retrieval system, or transmitted in any
form or by any means—electronic, mechanical, photocopying, recording, or
otherwise—without the prior written permission of Lerner Publishing Group,
Inc., except for the inclusion of brief quotations in an acknowledged review.

Lerner Publications Company
A division of Lerner Publishing Group, Inc.
241 First Avenue North
Minneapolis, MN 55401 U.S.A.

Website address: www.lernerbooks.com

Library of Congress Cataloging-in-Publication Data

Landau, Elaine.
    Boston terriers are the best! / by Elaine Landau.
      p.   cm. — (The best dogs ever)
    Includes index.
    ISBN 978-0-7613-5055-2 (lib. bdg. : alk. paper)
    1. Boston terrier—Juvenile literature. I. Title.
    SF429.B7L36 2011
    636.72—dc22   2009016421

Manufactured in the United States of America
1 — BP — 7/15/10

TABLE OF CONTENTS

CHAPTER ONE

A PEOPLE POOCH

Have you ever heard of a people person? That's someone who loves being around people. Usually these people are fun and friendly. You want to be with them.

Some dogs are like that too. You might call them people pooches. I know of a great one. It's smart, lively, and playful. This canine cutie even seems to have a sense of humor. It's the **Boston terrier.** These dogs are called Bostons or BTs for short.

Cute as Can Be

It's not hard to become a Boston fan. BTs are small, sturdy dogs. They stand from 15 to 17 inches (38 to 43 centimeters) tall at the shoulder. A BT can weigh up to 25 pounds (11 kilograms). That's about as much as a two-year-old child.

NAMING YOUR BT

A great dog needs a great name. Pick one that fits your pooch perfectly. Do any of these names seem just right?

Yankee

Bubbles

SPIKE

YODA

BiNGO

Socks

WAGS

Carley

Jake

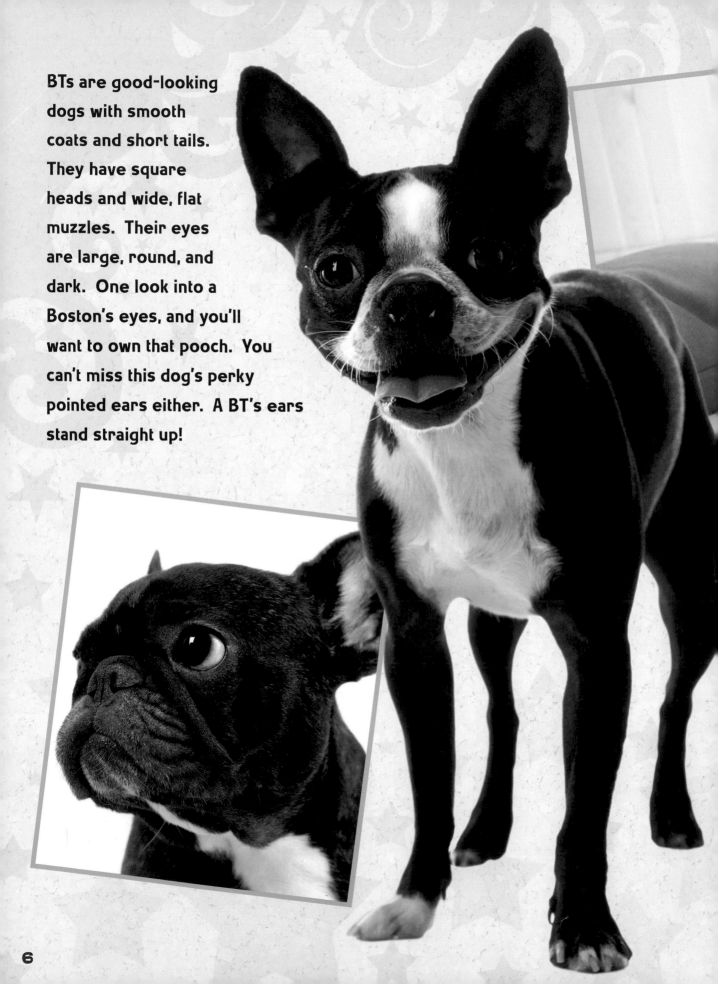

BTs are good-looking dogs with smooth coats and short tails. They have square heads and wide, flat muzzles. Their eyes are large, round, and dark. One look into a Boston's eyes, and you'll want to own that pooch. You can't miss this dog's perky pointed ears either. A BT's ears stand straight up!

Colorful Canines

Most BTs are black with white markings. They look like they are wearing tuxedos. These dogs seem to be dressed for a night out in only their fur!

BTs come in other colors too. They can be white and seal. Seal is a reddish black color. Other BTs are white and brindle. Brindle is a brown shade with black stripes.

The BT on the right is white and seal. The BT below has brindle markings.

A Perfect Pet

BTs want to be part of the family. They long to belong and tend to fit in well. They usually get along with children, older people, and other pets. The Boston terrier has often been called the American Gentleman because of its good manners and sweet personality. Their owners are sure they have the best dogs ever!

A STATE SYMBOL

Every state has symbols that represent it. These are some of the symbols of Massachusetts—the state in which Boston terriers were first bred:

The state berry is the cranberry.
The state bird is the black-capped chickadee.
The state dog is—you guessed it!—the Boston terrier.

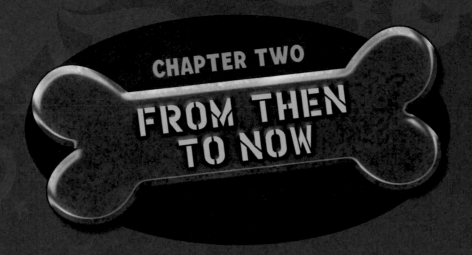

CHAPTER TWO
FROM THEN TO NOW

These days, BTs are gentle, friendly pooches. But in the late 1860s in Boston, Massachusetts, people bred these dogs for dogfights. Back then, BTs were bigger. Some weighed as much as 44 pounds (20 kg).

A woman sits with her BT around 1908. By this time, BTs were smaller, as they are today.

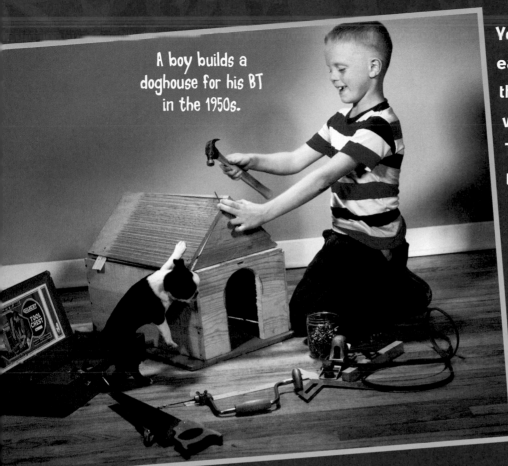

A boy builds a doghouse for his BT in the 1950s.

Yet even though early BTs were large, the dogs were not very good fighters. They were just too good-natured. People soon found another use for BTs. They saw that the pooches did well as pets. BTs became popular family dogs.

A PRESIDENTIAL POOCH

BTs are classy dogs. That may be why two U.S. presidents had them as pets. Warren G. Harding (right), our twenty-ninth president, had a BT. He named it Hub. Our thirty-eighth president, Gerald R. Ford, had two BTs as a child. Their names were Fleck and Spot.

BTs Today

BTs are still well-loved family dogs in modern times. Many people appreciate the breed's intelligence, good looks, and willingness to please. In fact, BTs are among the twenty most popular dog breeds in the United States.

What Type of Dog Is It?

The American Kennel Club (AKC) groups dogs by breed. Breeds that are alike in some ways are grouped together. Some of the AKC's groups are the sporting group, the working group, and the toy group. BTs are in the nonsporting group.

The komondor is part of the working group.

The Yorkshire terrier is part of the toy group.

The English springer spaniel is part of the sporting group.

Dogs in the nonsporting group are sturdy animals. They tend to be solid and squarely built. Yet these dogs do not all look alike.

The Tibetan terrier (*left*) and the dalmatian (*right*) are both in the nonsporting group.

A BT goes for a drive with its owner in the 1920s.

THE BARKING '20s

BTs were especially popular in the 1920s. At that time, about one-quarter of the dogs entered in dog shows were BTs!

Among dogs in the nonsporting group, the BT is special. It was the first breed in its group to be started in the United States. The Boston terrier is truly an all-American dog.

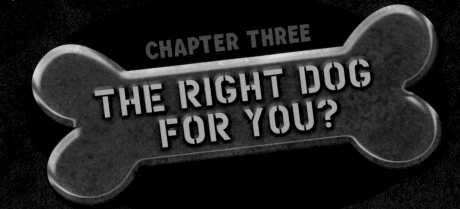

CHAPTER THREE

THE RIGHT DOG FOR YOU?

You see a BT and fall in love with it. You're sure you want one. You don't need to know anything more about the dog—or do you?

Rushing out to get any dog is never a good idea. Is a BT really a good match for you? Read on to find out.

BTs don't do well in places with extreme climates.

Here, There—but Not Everywhere

BTs live happily in both the country and the city. They are small enough to fit nicely in city apartments. Yet these dogs do not do well in areas where it is very cold or very hot.

A BT's short fur is not very warm. And like many dogs with flat muzzles, BTs can have trouble breathing in hot, humid places. So if you live in a place that has sizzling, steamy summers or frigid, snowy winters, think twice before getting a BT.

DRESS FOR SUCCESS

If you get a BT, buy it a sweater and some booties. This will help the pooch stay warm on cool days.

Do You Have Time for a People-Loving Pooch?

Your BT will always want to be with you. These friendly dogs cling to people like glue. This can make things sticky at times.

Do you have after-school activities on most days? Do you spend a lot of time out of the house? If so, a BT probably won't be right for you. These dogs are not loners.

BTs are happiest when they're cuddling with their owners.

Not a Dog for Couch Potatoes

BTs are lively little dogs. They enjoy going for walks and love to play. Would you rather play a video game than fetch? If this sounds like you, don't choose a BT. BT owners need plenty of energy for their dogs.

Head out to the backyard for a fun game of fetch with your BT!

BTs love to chew on sticks and toys.

Guess Who Likes to Chew?

All puppies chew on things. Yet BT puppies may do so more than most dogs. These puppies need lots of chew toys. Can your family afford to keep buying new dog toys? Find out before getting a BT.

Not a Watchdog

BTs will bark if someone comes too near the house. But they are not attack dogs. They are more likely to want to lick the thief! If you're looking for a watchdog, don't choose a BT.

Your BT probably won't chase away robbers. But it will always be ready to welcome you home!

Does a BT sound like the right dog for you? If so, you're lucky. A loving, fun dog is about to enter your life. Get ready to meet the best friend you'll ever have.

BT TRAINING

BTs learn quickly, and they love to make their owners happy. That makes BTs easy to train. Use praise and dog treats as rewards when training your dog.

CHAPTER FOUR

BE THE BEST DOG OWNER EVER

The big day is here at last! You're getting your new pooch. It's going to be a day you'll never forget.

Be Really Ready

Make sure things go smoothly. Buy some dog supplies ahead of time so your household will be BT-ready.

Not sure what you'll need to welcome Fido to your family? This basic list is a great place to start:

- collar

- leash

- tags (for identification)

- dog food

- food and water bowls

- crates (one for when your pet travels by car and one for it to rest in at home)

- treats (to be used in training)

- toys

An Important Stop

Also be sure to take your new dog to a veterinarian, or vet. That's a doctor who treats animals.

The vet will check your dog's health and give it the shots it needs. You'll see the vet again when your dog needs more shots. And you should take your dog to the vet if it becomes ill.

Grooming

Here's some good news: BTs are easy to groom. Brush your dog's coat every other day. If your dog gets dirty, wipe it down with a damp towel. Your BT will need a bath about every three months.

AN INDOOR DOG

Don't leave your BT alone in a fenced-in yard all day. BTs are not outdoor dogs. They need to be inside with the people they love.

Exercise and Play

Being active is important for your dog's health. Throw a ball to your BT, and it will happily bring it back to you. BTs love playing tug with a towel too. Trips to the park are fun outings for both you and your dog.

HEALTHFUL EATING

Don't feed your BT table scraps. You could end up with an overweight dog. Some human foods can also harm dogs. You may like chocolate, but it can be deadly for dogs.

Ask your vet how much food you should give your BT.

You and Your Best Friend

Make sure your dog gets the love and care it needs. Some days, you may be busy or tired. Yet your BT still needs to be fed, walked, and petted.

BTs are small dogs that are big on love. Your dog will always be there for you. Be there for your dog as well. The best dog ever should have the best owner ever.

Your BT will follow you anywhere!

GLOSSARY

American Kennel Club (AKC): an organization that groups dogs by breed. The AKC also defines the characteristics of different breeds.

breed: a particular type of dog. Dogs of the same breed have the same body shape and general features. *Breed* can also refer to producing puppies.

brindle: brown with black stripes. Some Boston terriers have white and brindle coats.

canine: a dog, or having to do with dogs

coat: a dog's fur

groom: to clean, brush, and trim a dog's coat

muzzle: a dog's nose, mouth, and jaws

nonsporting group: a group of many different types of dogs that are squarely built and sturdy. Dogs in the nonsporting group generally lack the characteristics of hunting dogs.

seal: a reddish black color. Some Boston terriers have white and seal coats.

veterinarian: a doctor who treats animals. Veterinarians are called vets for short.

FOR MORE INFORMATION

Books

Bozzo, Linda. *My First Dog.* Berkeley Heights, NJ: Enslow, 2008. This book offers readers some basic advice on dogs, including the best places to find a dog.

Brecke, Nicole, and Patricia M. Stockland. *Dogs You Can Draw.* Minneapolis: Millbrook Press, 2010. In this title especially for dog lovers, Brecke and Stockland show how to draw many different types of dogs.

Coren, Stanley. *Why Do Dogs Have Wet Noses?* Toronto: Kids Can Press, 2006. Read this selection for the answers to lots of fun questions about dogs. There's interesting info on how dogs hear, smell, and see the world.

Landau, Elaine. *Bulldogs Are the Best!* Minneapolis: Lerner Publications Company, 2010. Learn all about bulldogs—another very appealing and lovable dog in the nonsporting group.

Landau, Elaine. *Your Pet Dog.* Rev. ed. New York: Children's Press, 2007. This book is a good guide for young people on choosing and caring for a dog.

Websites

American Kennel Club

http://www.akc.org

Visit this website to find a complete listing of AKC-registered dog breeds, including the Boston terrier. The site also features fun printable activities for kids.

ASPCA Animaland

http://www2.aspca.org/site/PageServer?pagename=kids_pc_home

Check out this page for helpful hints on caring for a dog and other pets.

Index

Photo Acknowledgments

The images in this book are used with the permission of: © GK Hart/Vikki Hart/Photodisc/Getty Images, p. 4; © MIXA/Alamy, p. 5; © Inmagine/Alamy, p. 6 (left); © iofoto/Shutterstock Images, p. 6 (right); © Koki Iino/MIXA/Alamy, p. 7 (top), 22; © Big Cheese Photo LLC/Alamy, pp. 7 (bottom), 9 (top), 15, 18, 19 (right), 28 (top); © Datacraft-Sozaijiten/Alamy, p. 8 (top); © cynoclub/Shutterstock Images, p. 8 (bottom); © Geoff Hardy/Shutterstock Images, p. 9 (bottom); Library of Congress (LC-DIG-ggbain-03016), p. 10; © Harold M. Lambert/Hulton Archive/Getty Images, p. 11 (top); © Library of Congress/Getty Images, p. 11 (bottom); © Jessica Peterson/Getty Images, p. 12; © Tracy Morgan/Dorling Kindersley/Getty Images, p. 13 (top); © Erik Lam/Shutterstock Images, p. 13 (bottom left); © Eric Isselée/Dreamstime.com, p. 13 (bottom right); © Eric Isselée/Shutterstock Images, p. 14 (top both); © H. Armstrong Roberts/Retrofile/Getty Images, p. 14 (bottom); © Sparkling Moments Photography/Shutterstock Images, p. 16; © Dainis Derics/iStockphoto.com, p. 17 (top); © Andrea Rugg Photography/Beateworks/CORBIS, p. 17 (bottom); © Wendell Franks/iStockphoto.com, p. 19 (left); © John Kropewnicki/Shutterstock Images, p. 20 (top); © lumenphoto/iStockphoto.com, pp. 20 (bottom), 26; © Paul Wayne Wilson/PhotoStockFile/Alamy, p. 21; © Anderson Ross/Photodisc/Getty Images, p. 23 (top); © BIOS Bios-Auteurs Klein J.-L & Hubert M.-L./Peter Arnold, Inc., p. 23 (bottom); © Back in the Pack/Getty Images, p. 24; © Tooties/Dreamstime.com, p. 25 (top); © Uturnpix/Dreamstime.com, p. 25 (second from top); © orix3/iStockphoto.com, p. 25 (third from top); © Medvedev Andrey/Shutterstock Images, p. 25 (bottom); © Radius Images/Alamy, p. 27 (top); © Dempster Dogs/Alamy, p. 27 (bottom); © Fancy/Alamy, p. 28 (bottom); © Toshifumi Kitamura/AFP/Getty Images, p. 29 (top); © Jim Commentucci/Syracuse Newspapers/The Image Works, p. 29 (bottom).

Front cover: © Radius Images/Alamy.
Back cover: © Misti Hymas/Shutterstock Images.